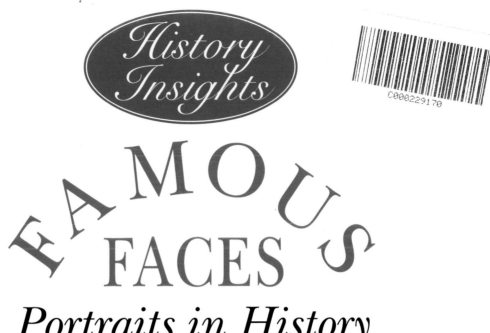

History Insights

FAMOUS FACES

Portraits in History

This book tells you about famous men and women in British history and shows how their portraits add to what we know about them.

Contents

Clare Gittings

National Portrait Gallery

Hodder & Stoughton

LONDON SYDNEY AUCKLAND

Henry VIII *King of England*

Henry VIII was the second Tudor king, following his father Henry VII. By the time this portrait was painted, Henry VIII was 45 years old and his three children, Mary, Elizabeth and Edward, had already been born. He had divorced his first wife, Catherine of Aragon. His second wife, Anne Boleyn, had been executed and his third wife, Jane Seymour, had died in childbirth. Now he was thinking about who to marry as his fourth wife. Henry had made himself head of the English Church instead of the Pope, so that he could divorce Catherine of Aragon.

This is a copy of a portrait of Henry by his court painter, a German called Hans Holbein. It is Holbein's picture that comes into most people's minds if you say 'Henry VIII'. Is this what you think of when someone says 'Henry VIII' to you?

This oil painting of Henry is very small, about the same size as a page of this book. At the same time, Hans Holbein also did a life-sized drawing of Henry VIII (see small picture). How has the position of Henry's arms changed from the drawing to the coloured painting? Hans Holbein wanted to show both Henry's hands in the oil painting.

◀ **Henry VIII after Hans Holbein**
(original painted c1536-1537)
Oil on copper, 27.9 × 20cm

◀ **Henry VIII with Henry VII** by Hans Holbein, 1536-1537 *Ink and watercolour on paper, 257.8 × 137.2cm*

PORTRAIT PUZZLE

Hans Holbein chose to show Henry without the usual signs of kingship, so he is not wearing a crown. How has he made Henry look rich? What words would you use to describe the expression on Henry's face?

Henry VIII	
1491	Born
1509	Crowned
1534	Act of Supremacy, making Henry Head of the Church of England
1536–1540	Dissolution of the Monasteries. Henry seized their lands and money for the crown.
1547	Died

Henry's wives
• Catherine of Aragon 1509-1533 (*divorced*)
• Anne Boleyn 1533-1536 (*executed*)
• Jane Seymour 1536-1537 (*died*)
• Anne of Cleves 1540 (*divorced*)
• Catherine Howard 1540-1542 (*executed*)
• Catherine Parr 1543-1547 (*survived*)

Sir Francis Drake
sailor and explorer

Sir Francis Drake was an Elizabethan sailor and explorer. Although he came from a poor family, he became a wealthy man. You can tell from his portrait that he is rich by his splendid clothes. Drake first went to sea when he was twelve. He was a pirate, attacking Spanish and Portuguese ships for their treasure.

Drake returned to England in 1580 and was knighted by Elizabeth I on board his ship, the *Golden Hind.* The portrait shows Drake wearing his court clothes for meeting the Queen, rather than his sailing clothes.

When Drake was knighted he was given a coat of arms (see small picture). God's hand is shown coming out of the clouds. What is God doing to Drake's ship? A Spanish sailor might not have agreed that Drake's ship was led by God!

Drake played an important part in helping to defeat the Spanish Armada when England was at war with Spain. There are many made-up stories about him. One is that he was playing a game of bowls as the Spanish Armada sailed up the English Channel. He finally died at sea.

▲ **Detail of shield** from **Sir Francis Drake** by an unknown artist.

PORTRAIT PUZZLE

In 1577 Drake set off on his most famous voyage. He was the first Englishman ever to sail right round the world. Can you find an object in the painting which suggests this?

◀ **Sir Francis Drake** by an unknown artist, c.1580-1585
Oil on panel, 181.3 x 113cm

Francis Drake	
1540	Born
1577–1580	Voyage round world
1581	Knighted
1587	Led successful raid on Cadiz, destroying Spain's supply-ships and delaying the Armada for a year.
1588	Fought against the Spanish Armada
1596	Died at sea during voyage to West Indies

Elizabeth I
Queen of England

Elizabeth I was the last Tudor monarch. Her mother, Anne Boleyn, was executed by her father, Henry VIII. Elizabeth herself never married but said that she was married to her country. The large portrait shows her wearing white, like a bride, and standing on a map of England.

Elizabeth I was 26 when she came to the throne (see small picture). When the big portrait was painted she was about 59 years old. In what way does her face look older than at her Coronation? Many of her teeth have fallen out and this has made her mouth look smaller.

◀ **Elizabeth I** by Marcus Gheeraerts the Younger, c.1592 *Oil on panel, 241.3 x 152.4cm*

▼ **Elizabeth I** by an unknown artist *Oil on panel, 127.3 x 99.7cm*

Much of her hair has also fallen out, so we are seeing a wig on her head.

The two types of weather in the picture show good times and bad times in Elizabeth's reign. There certainly were some dangerous moments. Rebels plotted to put her cousin Mary Queen of Scots on the throne. England went to war against Spain and Elizabeth's navy had to fight off the Spanish Armada. The artist has painted dark thunder-clouds behind Elizabeth to show that these troubles are now over. The sunshine in front of the queen suggests that the future will be bright and that the rest of her reign will be peaceful.

PORTRAIT PUZZLE

Elizabeth liked to call herself the 'moon goddess'. The large portrait shows her wearing both her favourite colour and her favourite jewel. Can you see what they are? How do they help her look like the moon? How does her make-up add to the effect?

Elizabeth I	
1533	Born
1554	Imprisoned in the Tower of London
1558	Crowned
1564	William Shakespeare, great English playwright, was born
1587	Mary Queen of Scots executed
1588	Spanish Armada defeated
1603	Died

▲ **Charles I and Sir Edward Walker** by an unknown artist,
Oil on canvas, 151.1 x 226.1cm

Charles I
King of Great Britain

Charles I was the second of the Stuart kings. He believed that he had been chosen by God to be King. Nothing would change his mind. He had many arguments with Parliament about who should rule the country. These led to the Civil War and finally to his trial and death by execution. There are several signs of war in this picture. How many can you find?

This portrait shows Charles with his secretary, Sir Edward Walker. Walker is writing down what the King says. Because Charles is shown standing, he looks taller and more important than his secretary. In fact Charles I was a very short man. The artist has flattered Charles by making him look taller. ('Flattery' is when you make people seem better than they really are.) The King's clothes are also richer - look at the two men's collars and cuffs. This picture was painted for Walker to hang in his house. The artist has also flattered the secretary by making him look very important to Charles.

The small picture is called a miniature - it is really this size. It shows Oliver Cromwell who fought against Charles in the Civil War and ruled England as Protector after Charles' execution. Cromwell believed in always telling the truth and would not let painters flatter him. He said he was to be painted 'warts and all'. Can you find the warts in his portrait? The portrait also shows that he is going bald.

Charles I	
1600	Born
1625	Crowned
1629–1640	Ruled without Parliament
1642–1646	First Civil War
1642	Charles I attempted to arrest five members of Parliament, but failed and had to flee London.
1645	New Model Army under Oliver Cromwell defeated Charles I's forces at Naseby.
1646–1648	Imprisoned by Parliamentarians
1648	Second Civil War
1649	Tried and executed
1653–1658	Oliver Cromwell ruled England as Lord Protector

▲ **Oliver Cromwell** attributed to Samuel Cooper, c.1655
Miniature on vellum, 6 x 4.8cm

Charles II
King of Great Britain

Charles II was the son of Charles I. He grew up in difficult and dangerous times. The Civil War began when he was 12 and led to the execution of his father in 1649.

Two years later Charles II tried to regain his kingdom at the battle of Worcester but he was defeated. To escape his enemies he had many adventures, including hiding in an oak tree (small picture) before fleeing abroad. When he finally came to the throne in 1660, Charles was a skilful ruler, but he preferred the pleasure of being king to the hard work of ruling the country.

The large portrait was painted in the last years of Charles's life. There are clues which tell us that he is King. Can you find the royal sceptre and the throne, which has carved angels holding a crown above his head?

The painter obviously had a problem with the King's right leg (the one nearest his sceptre). Look at this knee and go up the leg - does it join on to the body? A huge portrait like this would take several sittings to paint. It would not be easy for the artist to make sure that the person being painted was in exactly the same position every time.

◄ **Charles II and William Carlos in the Royal Oak** by Isaac Fuller, c.1660-1670 *Oil on canvas,* 206.1 x 315cm

PORTRAIT PUZZLE

The artist was not very skilful and has left some clues about how this picture was painted. Look at Charles's hands. Do they go with the face? The face is the king's but the clothes are being worn by someone else. Why do you think this was?

◄ **Charles II** attributed to Thomas Hawker, c.1680 *Oil on canvas, 226.7 x 135.6cm*

Charles II	
1630	Born
1642	Civil War begins
1649	Charles I executed
1651	Defeated at Worcester
1651–1660	Abroad
1660	Parliament asked Charles to return and take the throne as Charles II. This is known as the Restoration of the Monarchy.

Samuel Pepys *diary writer*

Samuel Pepys is famous for the diary which he kept during the first part of Charles II's reign. For most of his life Pepys worked for the Navy, organising supplies for the ships. His diary tells us a lot about life in London between 1660 and 1669. He lived through many important events such as the Great Plague of 1665. The next year Pepys brought the news of the Fire of London to the King.

Pepys wrote his diary in secret code so that his wife could not read it. This may be why Pepys did not choose to be shown holding his diary in his portrait. Instead he is holding a piece of music which he had written himself.

Pepys's diary tells us about how his portrait was painted (see extracts). Pepys visited the painter seven times and the picture took two months to complete. It was hard work sitting for the portrait, as he had to stay in an uncomfortable position. The diary also tells us that Pepys chose to hire a gown specially for his portrait, rather than wearing his own clothes. Why do you think he did this? What colour was the gown he hired?

17 March 1666 - This day I began to sit and he will make me, I think, a very fine picture. I do almost break my neck looking over my shoulder to make the posture for him to work by.

30 March 1666 - Sat till almost quite dark working upon my gown which I hired to be drawn in.

16 May 1666 - To Mr Hayls and paid him £14 for my picture. I am very well satisfied and took it in another coach home along with me and there with great pleasure my wife and I hung it up.

◀ **Samuel Pepys** by John Hayls, 1666
Oil on canvas, 75.6 x 62.9cm

Samuel Pepys	
1633	Born
1660	Begins diary
1665	Great Plague
1666	Fire of London
1669	Gave up writing diary due to bad eyesight
1672	Appointed Secretary to the Admiralty
1703	Died
1825	Diary decoded

▲ **Sir Joshua Reynolds,** self-portrait, c.1747
Oil on canvas, 63.5 x 74.3cm

Sir Joshua Reynolds
artist and portrait painter

Joshua Reynolds was a famous British painter who lived in the 18th century. While he was still at school Reynolds showed great talent for painting portraits. He was apprenticed to a portrait painter and later studied in Italy.

Joshua Reynolds painted this self-portrait when he was about 24 years old. It shows him at work with his brushes, palette and canvas.

In one year, Joshua Reynolds painted more than 150 people's portraits. To do this many he had to use other artists to paint the less important parts, such as the clothes and backgrounds.

Joshua Reynolds was interested in the training of artists and the study of art. He helped to set up the Royal Academy of Arts in London and was its first president.

The small picture is a self-portrait by another great 18th century artist, Thomas Gainsborough. He liked painting landscapes showing the countryside, rather than doing portraits. Even his self-portrait has trees in the background. However, Gainsborough painted portraits because people liked to have pictures of themselves and it was a better way to earn a living.

◀ **Self-portrait** by Thomas Gainsborough, c.1759
Oil on canvas, 76.2 x 63.5cm

PORTRAIT PUZZLE

What would you use to help you paint a picture of yourself? What do you think Reynolds is looking at so carefully? He was interested in the effects of light and shade. Where is the light coming from in this picture? How has he made the shade?

Joshua Reynolds	
1723	Born in Plymouth, Devon
1740–1743	Apprenticed under portraitist Thomas Hudson
1750–1752	Studied in Rome, Italy
1768	Became first President of the Royal Academy
1769	Knighted
1792	Died

Admiral Horatio Nelson
naval commander

Horatio Nelson was a famous naval commander. His victories during the Napoleonic Wars, between Britain and France, made him a national hero. Nelson had this portrait painted for his girlfriend, Emma Hamilton (see small picture). It shows him at the end of the Battle of the Nile in 1798. The French commander has surrendered and has sent Nelson his sword, wrapped in the French flag.

The artist was not actually on the ship, painting this picture at the time of the battle. As well as this portrait, there are written reports of the battle by people who fought in it. The account below is based on these.

Nelson was wounded above his right eye and was suddenly covered in blood. 'I am killed', he said, 'remember me to my wife'.

In fact the wound was not deep and was bandaged by the ship's surgeon. Shortly after midnight the French Admiral's sword was brought to Nelson by the first lieutenant of the ship. At sunrise it became clear how fierce the battle had been. A sailor later remembered:

'An awful sight it was. The whole bay was covered with dead bodies.' The ships were badly damaged. On the day after the battle the sailors had to scrub the blood off the decks.

PORTRAIT PUZZLE

What are the differences between the picture and the written evidence? The picture tries to show Nelson in a good light, and makes it seem as if he won the battle easily. Can you see any sign of Nelson's wound or the dead bodies? Why do you think that the picture hides the truth? Nelson was a very short man. Can you explain why the Lieutenant has been changed to a young midshipman in the picture?

► **Lady Emma Hamilton** by George Romney, c.1785 *Oil on canvas, 62.2 x 54.6cm*

◄ **Horatio Nelson, Viscount Nelson with a midshipman** by Guy Head, 1798-1800 *Oil on canvas, 222.9 x 168.9cm*

Horatio Nelson	
1758	Born
1770	Joined Navy
1794	Lost eye in Corsica
1797	Knighted
1798	Lost arm
1798	Won Battle of the Nile and destroyed France's naval power in the Mediterranean.
1801	Made Viscount
1805	Killed at Battle of Trafalgar. He is buried in St Paul's Cathedral.

Queen Victoria
Queen of the United Kingdom

In the whole history of Britain, Queen Victoria is the monarch who has reigned for the longest time. However, when Victoria first came to the throne she had to overcome a number of problems. She was only 18 years old and was quite small, only about 1.5 metres tall. Also, Britain had not had a woman ruler for over a hundred years. Portraits like this helped to show people that she was powerful and would be able to cope with the job of ruling the country. Victoria's face looks strong and determined. The artist has used the flowing robes to make her look taller. There are various signs that she rules England - roses, lions and the red cross of St George. Can you find these in the picture? The Tudor roses are for England and Wales. On her cloak there are also shamrocks for Ireland and thistles for Scotland.

In fact Victoria reigned for 64 years. By her death she was ruling an Empire so large that it was said that the sun never set on it.

Victoria never got over the death of her husband, Prince Albert, in 1861. The small portrait shows her many years after he had died, and tells us that she is still remembering him. She is dressed in black, the colour of mourning, and wears a brooch and a bracelet with Albert's picture. She is holding a handker-chief which suggests that she might have been crying. Do you think that she looks sadder than in the earlier portrait?

◀ **Queen Victoria** by Lady Julia Abercromby after Heinrich von Angeli, 1883 (original painted 1875) *Watercolour, 145.7 x 97.8cm*

◀ **Queen Victoria** by Sir George Hayter, 1863 (replica of portrait of 1838) *Oil on canvas, 285.8 x 179cm*

Queen Victoria	
1819	Born
1837	Became Queen on the death of her uncle, William IV.
1840	Married her cousin Prince Albert
1851	Great Exhibition held
1861	Albert died of typhoid
1876	Made Empress of India
1897	Diamond Jubilee. Rulers came from all over the world to show their support.
1901	Died

The Brontë sisters   *writers*

The Brontë sisters, Anne, Emily and Charlotte, wrote some of the best-known novels of the Victorian age.

They lived in Yorkshire with their father who was a vicar. Early Victorians felt that women should not be writers, so the three sisters had to give themselves men's names to get their books published.

This portrait of the Brontë sisters was painted by their brother Branwell. He was not an artist. Because he had trouble painting hands he has hidden his sisters' hands behind the desk. He was also not very good at faces. The Brontës look very flat in their portrait. The portrait of the writer Charles Dickens (small picture) makes him look far more like a real person.

The portrait of Dickens was used in his book Nicholas Nickleby to show readers what the author looked like. The portrait of the Brontës could not be used in their books because it would have given away the fact that they were women.

The Brontë sisters' books sold very well. When people found out that the authors were women, it helped to change Victorian ideas about what women could do.

▶ **Charles Dickens** by Daniel Maclise, 1839
Oil on canvas, 91.4 x 71.4cm

PORTRAIT PUZZLE

Some things have happened to the Brontës' portrait since it was painted. Can you see the lines on it? It has obviously been folded at some time. Look carefully at the lighter strip between Emily and Charlotte. Can you find a head in it? It seems that at first Branwell put himself into the picture but later painted himself out again. Perhaps he felt he did not deserve to be in the painting, as he had not been as successful as his sisters.

◀ **The Brontë Sisters** by Patrick Branwell Brontë, c.1834 *Oil on canvas, 90.2 x 74.6cm*
Left to right: Anne, Emily, Charlotte

The Brontë sisters	
1816	Charlotte born
1818	Emily born
1820	Anne born
1846	The sisters published *Poems by Currer, Ellis and Acton Bell*
1847	Charlotte's *Jane Eyre* published
1848	Emily's *Wuthering Heights* published
1848	Emily and Branwell died of tuberculosis
1849	Anne died of tuberculosis
1855	Charlotte died during pregnancy

Isambard Kingdom Brunel
engineer

Isambard Kingdom Brunel was a famous engineer, like his father who was French. By the age of 20, Isambard was already helping his father build the first tunnel under the River Thames in London. For the Great Western Railway he built bridges, viaducts and tunnels, but he is also famous for building the Clifton Suspension Bridge and designing steamships.

The largest of these ships was the *Great Eastern*. The photograph was taken at the first launch of the *Great Eastern* in 1857. The chains suggest the enormous size of the ship. The *Great Eastern* was five times the size of any ship afloat.

Brunel has not dressed up for his photograph. He is wearing ordinary work clothes and his shoes and trouser legs are muddy. The picture shows that he is the kind of person who does not mind hard work and getting his hands dirty.

In the same year Brunel had his portrait painted by a friend (small picture). Where did he choose to be painted? The picture shows the pencil and paper he would use to plan and design bridges, tunnels and ships. Which do you think gives a better idea of Brunel, the photograph or the painting?

The first launch of the *Great Eastern* was a disaster and it was not till the next year that Brunel finally managed to get his ship afloat. He died soon afterwards, worn out by worry.

◄ **Isambard Kingdom Brunel** by Robert Howlett, November 1857
Albumen print, 28.6 x 22.5cm

▲ **Isambard Kingdom Brunel** by John Callcott Horsley, 1857, *Oil on canvas, 91.4 x 70.5cm*

Isambard Kingdom Brunel	
1806	Born
1826	Engineer for the Thames Tunnel
1831	Designed the Clifton Suspension Bridge
1833–1859	Engineer to the Great Western Railway
1837	Designed the *Great Western* steamship
1852–1858	Designed the *Great Eastern* steamship
1859	Died
1864	Clifton Suspension Bridge completed

▲ **The Mission of Mercy: Florence Nightingale receiving the wounded at Scutari** by Jerry Barrett, c.1856, *Oil on canvas 141 x 212.7cm*

Florence Nightingale
founder of modern nursing

Florence Nightingale is famous for her work as a nurse. She grew up in a wealthy family. The small picture shows her when she was about 16, sitting sewing with her older sister. Her family were horrified when she refused to marry and went to train as a nurse instead.

During the Crimean War, Florence Nightingale volunteered to lead a team of women to nurse the sick and wounded soldiers at Scutari, where she earned the name of 'the lady with the lamp'. The building in the large picture is an old army barracks which they had to use as a hospital. Can you see the buildings with the tall towers through the archway? They are mosques, which gives us a clue that they are in Turkey.

Florence Nightingale found the army medical services in chaos. She organised the hospital properly and saved many soldiers' lives by giving them good food and dressing their wounds.

On her return to Britain, Florence Nightingale founded the modern profession of nursing. For the last fifty years of her life she was an invalid but went on working from her bed.

▲ **Florence Nightingale with her sister, Frances Parthenope** by William White, c.1836
Watercolour, 45.1 x 34.9cm

PORTRAIT PUZZLE

This picture shows wounded soldiers arriving at the hospital entrance. What makes it easy to see the soldiers in the crowd? How has the artist used the light to make Florence Nightingale stand out from all the other people?

Florence Nightingale	
1820	Born
1851	Trained as a nurse
1853	Appointed nursing superintendent in London
1854–1856	Nursed in the Crimea
1860	Founded the Nightingale School of Nursing at St Thomas' Hospital
1861	Became an invalid
1907	First woman to get Order of Merit
1910	Died

Amy Johnson *pioneer of flying*

Amy Johnson was a British pilot who became famous with her solo flight from London to Darwin, Australia. Before this she had been a secretary and the furthest she had flown was from London to Hull. Her flight to Darwin took 19 days and, though it did not break any records, it made her very popular. The newspapers called her the 'Queen of the Air'. However, her flight from Siberia to Tokyo did set a record and her flight from London to Cape Town broke the record for solo flying. When the Second World War started, she worked for the Air Ministry delivering planes to airfields. She disappeared on one of these flights.

What signs of flying can you find in Amy Johnson's photograph? We can see by her flying jacket, hat and goggles that she is a pilot, but the photographer has made her look more like a film star. He shows her wearing make-up in a close-up pose, taken in the photographer's studio rather than on an airfield.

▲ **Robert Falcon Scott** by Herbert Ponting, 7 October 1911 *Toned bromide print, 35.4 x 45.5cm*

The small photograph shows another pioneer, the explorer Captain Scott, writing his journal in 1911 in his winter quarters in the Antarctic. This photographer has not tried to alter Scott to make him look more exciting or glamorous. The room is untidy and Scott is wearing his everyday clothes. He is not even looking up from his journal. It is a much more realistic photograph than the one of Amy Johnson. Scott never came back from this expedition to the South Pole, but died on the return journey in 1912.

Amy Johnson	
1903	Born
1928	Given pilot's licence
1930	Solo flight London to Australia
1931	Solo flight Siberia to Tokyo
1932	Solo flight London to Cape Town
1936	Flew the Atlantic with her husband, Jim Mollison
1939	Second World War started
1941	Disappeared flying

◀ **Amy Johnson** by J. Capstack, c.1933-1935 *Toned bromide print, 20 x 14.6cm*

Sir Winston Churchill
politician

Sir Winston Churchill played a major part in many of the important events of the 20th century. He is most famous for his strong leadership of Britain during the Second World War. He became Prime Minister in May 1940 as Hitler's armies were invading Europe.

When he was elected he said, 'I have nothing to offer but blood, toil, tears and sweat'. He is still remembered today for the stirring speeches that he made to keep the British people confident during the difficult wartime years.

The photograph below was taken in the same year as Churchill became Prime Minister and was made into a postcard at the time. During the war it was important to have a strong leader. People needed to know what he looked like, and not many people had televisions at that time.

In his spare time, Churchill took painting lessons from the artist who painted the large portrait. When photography was first developed, it looked as if it might put portrait painters out of business. In fact, photography brought new freedom to artists. They no longer had to paint exactly what people looked like, because photographs could do that. Instead they could concentrate on showing personality in their portraits.

PORTRAIT PUZZLE

In what ways are the painting and photograph of Churchill similar? One difference between the two is the amount of background. Which makes Churchill seem 'larger than life', do you think? Another difference is that the photograph has light and shade while the painting uses patches of different colour. Some of the colours are quite surprising if you look closely - how many colours can you find?

▲ **Sir Winston Spencer Churchill** by Sir Cecil Beaton, 1940 *Bromide print, 23.7 x 19cm*

◄ **Sir Winston Churchill** by Walter Richard Sickert, 1927 *Oil on canvas, 45.7 x 30.5cm*

Sir Winston Churchill	
1874	Born
1900	Elected to Parliament
1911–1915	First Lord of the Admiralty
1914–1918	First World War. In 1915 he joined the army and fought in France.
1939–1945	Second World War
1940–1945 and 1951-1955	Prime Minister
1953	Won the Nobel Prize for Literature. His writings include The Second World War and *A History of the English-Speaking Peoples*.

Margaret Thatcher
first woman Prime Minister

History is being made all the time. The events we read about in our newspapers today will become the history of the future. Both the women shown on these pages have made history in recent years.

Margaret Thatcher was the first woman to become Prime Minister of Great Britain. This portrait was painted at 10 Downing Street, the Prime Minister's home. The large room, grand furniture, chandelier and portraits show that it is an important place. This portrait took two years to paint and the artist visited Margaret Thatcher about ten times. Does she look friendly or stern in this picture? She was sometimes known by the nickname of 'The Iron Lady'.

Diane Abbot (small picture) was the first black woman to become a British Member of Parliament. The photographer suggests that Diane Abbot is on the ladder to success by the background she has chosen for her picture.

◀ **Margaret Hilda Thatcher, Baroness Thatcher** by Rodrigo Moynihan, 1984
Oil on canvas, 126.5 x 101.5cm

▲ **Diane Abbot** by Miriam Reik, 1986
Colour cibachrome print, 35.8 x 29.3cm

Margaret Thatcher	
1926	Born
1959	Elected Member of Parliament
1975	Elected Leader of the Conservative Party
1979, 1983 and 1987	Elected Prime Minister
1988	Became longest serving Prime Minister of this century
1990	Resigned as Prime Minister
1992	Entered House of Lords

What about you? What will you do in the future? Perhaps you, too, will make history and your portrait will hang in the National Portrait Gallery.

Even if you do not become famous, you will always be important to your family and friends and your photograph will matter to them.

Next time you have your picture taken, think about what you could tell people about yourself. The clothes you wear, the way you pose, the background of the photograph and objects you choose to put in the picture all say something about you.

Historians in the future might then use your picture to find out more about you, just as you have used the portraits in this book to find out about famous people in the past.

Index

British Library Cataloguing in Publication Data
Gittings, Clare
  Famous Faces: Portraits in History
  (History Insights Series)
  I. Title II. Series
  920.042
  ISBN 0 340 59570 1
Copyright © 1994 National Portrait Gallery

Published by Hodder and Stoughton Children's Books, a division of Hodder Headline plc, 338 Euston Road, London NW1 3BH.
Printed in Hong Kong by Colorcraft.

The right of Clare Gittings to be identified as the author of this work has been asserted by her in accordance with Copyright, Design and Patents Act 1988.

First Published in Great Britain 1994 10 9 8 7 6 5 4 3 2 1